Farm Fantasies and Figments of Imagination

By James L. Baumann

Printed in The United States of America
Link Printing, Groveland, Florida 34736

No part of this publication may be reproduced in whole or in part, or stored in a retrieval system, or transmitted in any form or by any means, electronic, mechanical, photocopying, recording, or otherwise, without written permission from the publisher. For information regarding permission, write to Post Mortem Publications, 146 East Broad Street, Groveland, FL 34736, or E-Mail: Contact@Postmortempublications.com

ISBN 978-1-941880-07-4

Copyright: ©Post Mortem Publications 2014
All rights reserved

~ First Edition ~

Snowflakes

I love the snow; it's made of tiny souls
Crystallized in flakes from angel tears
They're young and old and do behold
The thoughts of everyone in silence
While quietly they float about in time
Sublime in purity and immune to woe

Falsely, they're not driven by the wind
As if the wind controls their destiny
For souls exist wherever souls exist
Their presence be not tangible to see
They are the essence of a snowflake
A commodity worth nothing in the air
Except for children's noses to discover
And memories of other cherished times
These nano souls appear and reappear
And year to year they seem to reaffirm
They do not melt away when touched
They just become a part of us as such

- J. L. Baumann

Contents

Enchantment 2
Beezilla 4
Flight School 6
The Fortunes of Faith 8
The Milk of Kindness 10
Ogden Bath 12
Survival of the Slowest 14
Bon Voyage 16
The Funny Farm 18
Good Morning 20
Guests 22
An Amicable Resolution 24
Baaa'd Deal 25
Horse Sense 26
Graduation 28
Elephant Farming 30
The No Bell Bull 32
Secretly Enchanted 34
Grace Embraced 36
Regal Grace 38
Natural Predators 40
Farm Time 42
Oh, For the Love of Spud 44
Gander This 46
Eat Firebrand Chickens 48
The Hunk of Funk 50
A Blessed Spirit 52
Malaise 53

Enchantment

The fairy folks all call me Shaun
And mischief is my middle name
Catch me quick before I'm gone
And all my riches you can claim

In clover fields I'm found to be
As fluffy clouds appear at dawn
Trust me magic and you will see
Where are the fairies do belong

Enchanted trees sway breezily
To silver lyres with dulcet song
As rainbows call you teasingly
To just submit and come along

To dream on tuffets of chiffon
And interface with leprechauns

Beezilla

I am the queen of dragon bees
And yes, there are such things
We're fiercely tiny little beings
Flying in the summer's breeze
We do just what we please

I buzz, I do not whoosh about
Flapping big and clumsy wings
Upsetting flowers in the spring
And belching fire out my snout
As only tiny sparks fly out

I do not have a ponderous tail
To go the get myself ensnared
Entangled then, in desprataire
And wrangled up, to no avail
My stinger would prevail

Tiny scales of yellow and black
Add armour to my composition
In total fearsome recognition
So knowing we attack in packs
You better guard your necks

We oversee the bumblebees
And honey bees, our specialty
So if you say you don't believe
In all those little dragon bees
Attack the bees, - I guarantee

I will bring you to your knees

Flight School

Don't throw in the towel, said the wise old owl
If nothing is ventured, then nothing is gained
To have an adventure, and not run afoul
You need to fly right, and you need to be trained

As the little bird listened, his eyes opened wide
His feathers a flutter, he danced all around
When he couldn't decide, he got queasy inside
And worried to death that he'd fall to the ground

He looked down below, the tree was so high
The branches were there to ruin his flight
He looked up above, there was nothing but sky
But felt in his soul he did not have it right

He then cautiously went to the edge of the nest
And finally was met with a rear-ended boot
While flapping about, he passed his first test
While all the time thinking his teacher's a brute

He flitted and floated, not far did he roam
And struggled profusely to stay in the air
Endeavored he fought to make it back home
To once again have the security there

He landed exhausted, and he slipped and he fell
As he flew through the nest like a bat out of hell
He realized then, there was no other route
And the stoic old coot - really did give a hoot

The Fortunes of Faith

You can't hide from me, the wise old Shaman said
For I am your reality, when I'm inside your head
You think you're all alone, when no one is around
But surely it is known, I can move without a sound

Sometimes I am a twitch, that cannot be explained
Sometimes I am that itch, that drives us all insane
Perchance I am the spirit, that treats you in despair
Perhaps you cannot hear it, but feel that I am there

I'm also there in happiness, escorting your elation
Abating all your sadness, by instilling inspiration
To see beyond the trivial, to all that is worthwhile
And be beyond the physical, the essence of a smile

So dream a dream worth catchin, in quiet solitude
And I'll reward your passion, at our next interlude

The Milk of Kindness

I don't know what to do
I practiced my best moo
I even swat the flies away

I'm docile and subdued
And have a gentle mood
And I hardly ever stray

I always see this through
And give my best to you
But candidly I have to say

At the risk of being bold
Your hands are oh so cold
So warm them first today

Okay?

Ogden Bath

It is to laugh
When in the bath
You have your rubber duck

You splash about
Get water up your snout
And in the drain your toe is stuck

The bubbles are what hide
Your wounded pride
With any luck

Your fantasies abound
In a realm that you have found
That doesn't suck

Your singing's such a wonder
That angels put asunder
You're very soul to pluck

The elusive soap escapes
As soapy mountains make
Imagination run amuck

But the only thing that's real
That you can truly feel
In that insipid rubber duck

Survival of the Slowest

So, I'm an old goat
So what
And you're an old cow

As barnyard friends
I cannot disavow
We love to live together

My head is strong
You plod along
And live to see another day

Down here upon the farm

Bon Voyage

    The   now
        Attic
      Pussycats
It has wooden a floor
This time the trunk is back
Three new stickers naturally
Black behind brass hinges
Locked up and secure
Safe from the cats
Party time!
     T   d
    a   n
   i   e
  l s

The Funny Farm

They call me Quackie
But don't get alarmed
I'm just slightly wackie
Down here on the farm

They say I belong here
But what do they know
It's them who're in fear
Over where I might go

They say that I toddle
And think I'll fall down
But it's really a waddle
I'm a duck, not a clown

Good Morning

A tweet tweet, a woof woof, a peep peep, and a moo moo!
The animals are all about but where in heaven's name are you?
Still in your bed with silly dreams that dance inside your head
In poppy fields that help you push up daisies when you're dead

Apple, peach, and cherry pie just doesn't fall right from the sky
And cows and horses don't discuss the nature of the pesky fly
As chickens don't lay scrambled eggs, drenched in hollandaise
And steers don't sire hamburgers, all served with mayonnaise

Pizza isn't picked from pepperoni trees, free with extra cheese
And cotton candy isn't spun by black and yellow bumble bees
The chocolate peanut butter cups will never really ever bloom
While graham cracker generals order s'mores to march in tune

But fantasies need sustenance, a natural call to live and thrive
For farms neglected or unattended, will kill the animals inside

Guests

As Jack Frost skates on rural lanes
And Frosty rules a snow's domain
While Old Man Winter freezes rain
You think of springtime once again

When little fairies flit and fly
As farmers sow their corn and rye
The dormant spirits come alive
To play in rushing brooks nearby

As summer trees shade Elvin Kings
An errant Bard gives song to things
That o'er the farm and fields do ring
Of all the cheer their harvest brings

When orange leaves begin to fall
'Forget us not' - the fairies call
Our spirits big, tho we be small
And we'll return to dust you all

So don't be sad, it's not the end
For soon you will see Jack again

An Amicable Resolution

Independence is my name and surely all the same
I'm packaged differently as you can plainly see
For I'm the incarnation of impunity

Don't think you can command or even reprimand
My nature to abide to rules you have prescribed
To try to subjugate my pride

I'm capable of everything and do most anything
It's inherent that I pounce upon the errant Mouse
For tenacity it me, ounce for ounce

Okay, so I am finicky, indeed perhaps persnickety
But for a special treat, a loving culinary feat
I'll pretend to be your Cat Elite

Baaaa'd Deal

Don't want to get fleeced?
Don't act like a sheep!

Horse Sense

A good horse has the sense to not distinguish
The difference between a bribe and a reward
Whenever it is fed a carrot
After all, -It tastes the same regardless

Graduation

And so pell-mell they all went into hell
With righteous good intentions.
We watched 'em leave and wished them well
As products of our own invention.

And so, oh well, as farmers in the dell
We stay behind, our fates have been decided.
To watch them leave, yet still compelled
To have their needs provided.

We sit and wait a spell, to listen for the bell
That rings anticipating their return.
We watched them leave and bid farewell
To the very soul of our concerns.

To plant a seed and watch it grow,
Is the greatest joy that one can know.

Elephant Farming

Oh where, oh where, has my elephant gone?
And where would he go; it's here he belonged
I thought he was happy right here on my farm
Surely you've seen him; he's as big as my barn

Now I fed him and fed and fed him again
And sometimes I thought, it just wouldn't end
So I plowed all day long, working into the night
And sometimes I felt there was no end in sight

And for year after year I had struggled along
So where, oh where, has my elephant gone?
I thought he was happy down here on the farm
He was one of the family, and now I'm alarmed

Now I shall never forget, the day he came here
I was thirty years younger, not thinking so clear
Now the elephant said, I am just what you need
But neglected to tell me the price of the feed

Still a bargain's a bargain, and I held up my end
And 'tho he deceived me, I thought him a friend
Oh where, oh where, has my elephant strayed?
He just disappeared as my mortgage was paid!

The No Bell Bull

I'm strong and I'm mighty
A thing to behold
So don't take me lightly
Even when I get old

As long as I'm standing
You should be in fear
For I am commanding
This pasture right here

I'm sure not a cow
And I sure ain't a steer
So respectfully bow
To this bull standing here

Secretly Enchanted

I'm mystical and magical, a wonder to behold
But only true believers, can see me I am told
Often just the little ones can see me in the air
But if you look quite carefully, surely I am there

For I'm secretly enchanted, forbidden to tell you my name
For if I do I'll disappear, - and you'll never see me again

Sometimes I hide in meadows green, behind the willow trees
Sometimes I just appear to be the wind you cannot see
I flit and fly like a butterfly and dance atop the clover
And leave no trace of being there, and then I do it over

For I'm secretly enchanted, forbidden to tell you my name
For if I do I'll disappear, - and you'll never see me again

I can ride upon a rainbow, - high above the ground
I can heal a heart's unhappiness, with smiles I have found
And if you feed me apples and other things delicious
And pet my nose and brush my hair, - I will grant you wishes

So if you're ever lonely, and feeling all forlorn
Just think of me - and you will see - a precious unicorn

But I'm secretly enchanted, forbidden to tell you my name
For if I do I'll disappear, - and you'll never see me again

Grace Embraced

I'm soft and I'm furry and I'm not in a hurry
The little bunny said to me
I won't even struggle when I get a snuggle
As verily soft as soft can be
But carrots beware of this ravenous hare
I'll eat you most deliciously
And as you well know, we all have to go
Really, not much differently
So whenever I lunch on carrots a bunch
I do completely reverently
See I knew all along, my carcass belonged
To the local glove factory

Regal Grace

I am the show of shows, the thoroughbred had said
For everyone does know, the reason why I'm bred
I'm beautiful to look at, and raced because I'm fast
The people often bet their hats, I'd never finish last

I'm fed the best of oats, and I'm curried every day
I am the toast of all the folks, a magnificent display
I'm trotted out for all to see, myself in all my glory
To justify, most splendidly, an investor's inventory

I know I am expendable, a daily fact I have to face
And it is not contestable, eventually I'll lose a race
So every time I'm harnessed, a victim of my reign
Just like a trophy tarnished, I bear this unashamed

It's said, it is my heart, that makes me run this way
I say I walk up to the start, to only live another day

Natural Predators

I'm just a little firefly that's trying to stay alive
It isn't hard to understand
Just why I fly at night

When all the birdies of the day are finally asleep
I take my lantern out to play
Lighting up the street

So happily I fly along to brighten up the night
Not fearing to be eaten now
While I am in mid flight

But my light is not forever, as is moon and stars
Knowing I might be entrapped
By little kids with jars

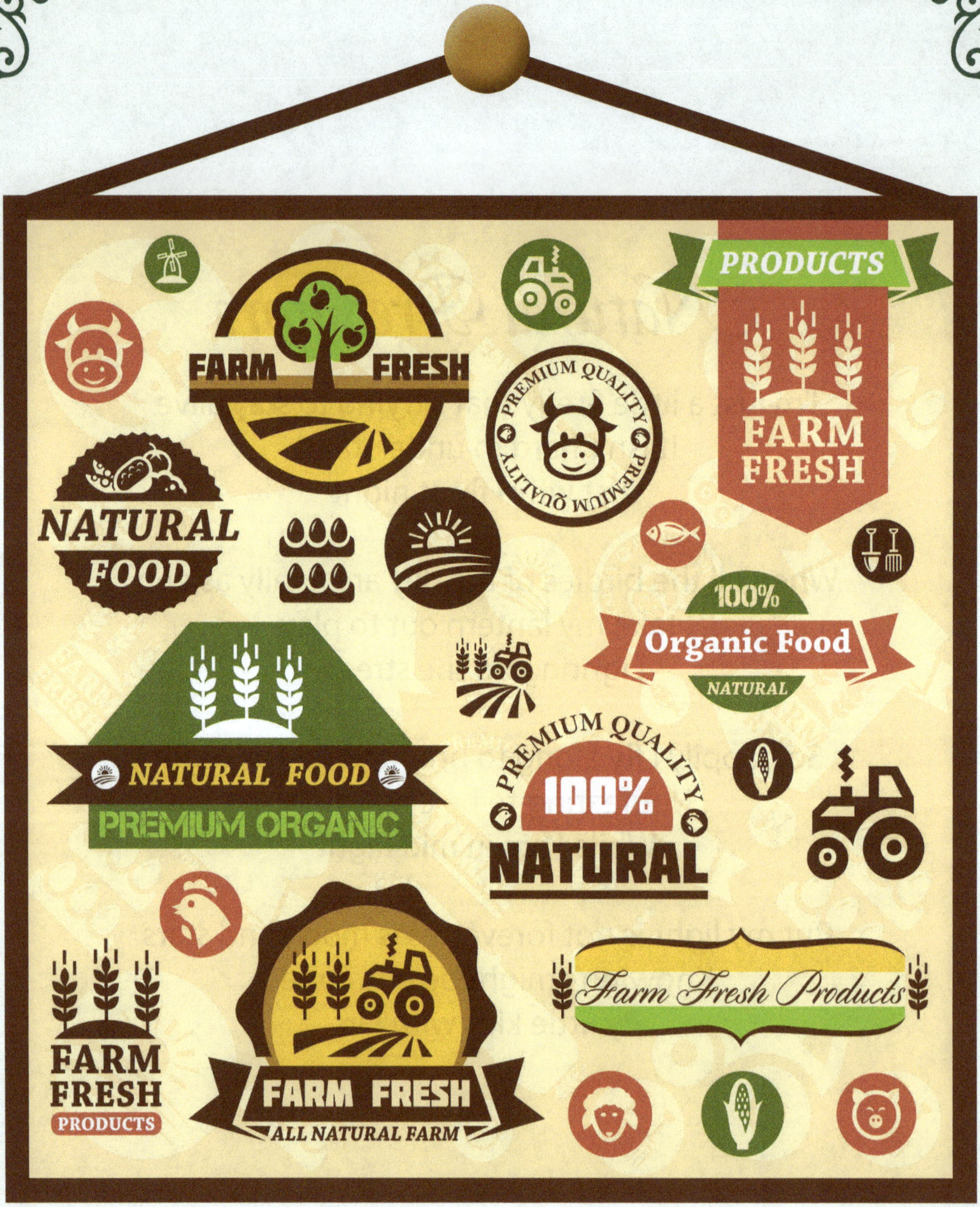

Farm Time

I think there's a pudding made by figs
And baseball gloves are made by pigs
As chickens make the scrambled eggs
The strong oak trees make table legs
And hereford cows make juicy steaks
While jelly's made by concord grapes
As sheep make blankets for our beds
Straw makes hats to keep our heads
I think one makes too many mistakes
Not making the needed time it takes

To understand where it comes from

Oh, For the Love of Spud

Everybody loves a good potato
At holidays you eat them mashed
You can fix them on your plate so
You can eat them unabashed

Some people build a gravy dam
And work to manage it with skill
To keep its essence from the yam
And o'er the corn it would spill

Potato dams do serve quite well
To engineer the things you savor
The gravy you can always tell
Enhances the potato's flavor

So now you're stuffed, to no surprise
You dream of ketchup on your fries

Gander This

The goose of imagination, pleaded kill me not
For I will lay forever, and I control all thought
Killing me is fruitless, and realistically unwise
For the eggs if inspiration, deep within me lie

Chickens lay a lot of eggs, in cartons I am told
A regulated product, and clinically controlled
They lay them by the numbers, quite efficiently
And mechanically perform, without sagacity

Now turkeys lay some eggs, a quality to note
But knowledge isn't something they promote
Their beautiful to look at, and visually a treat
But are sadly in the end, just a piece of meat

It's lonely at the top, without some intellect
And to kill the golden goose, you will regret

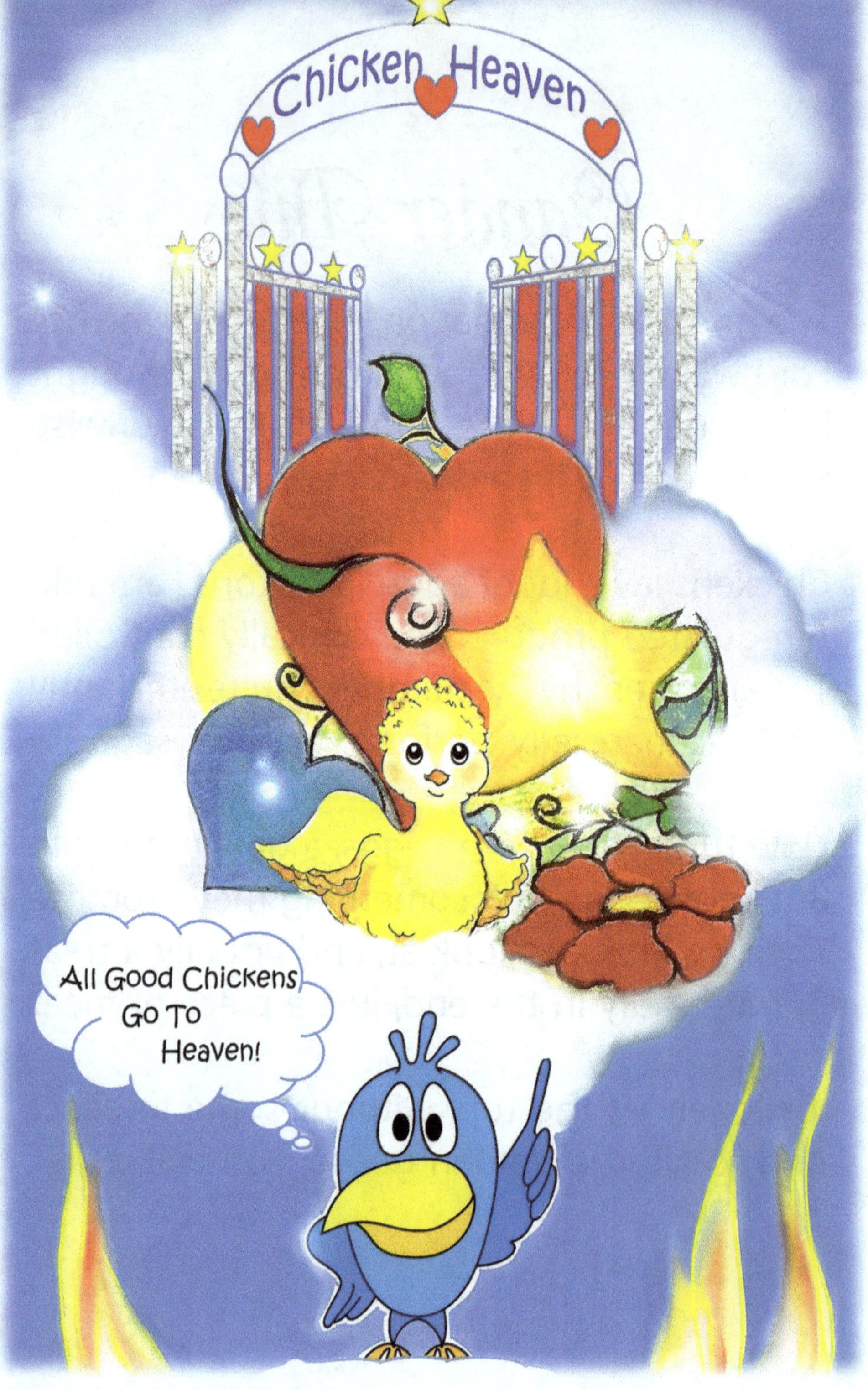

Eat "Firebrand" Chickens

Do chickens have a soul, the preacher asked his flock?
And know the end is near, as they're put inside a crock?
And so my feathered friends, what do you have to say?
I guess it all depends, did you confess your sins today?

Some chickens run away, quite terrified in mortal fear!
As I submit to you today, they knew the end was near!
Gorged to death on feed, they didn't say their prayers!
Then finally they understood the meaning of prepared!

It's not about your dinner, with carrots, corn, and peas!
It's boiling broth for you, whenever God ain't pleased!
So you have to ask yourself, do chickens have a soul?
Are you prepared to testify, that chickens do not know?

And now the question is, -do *I* have a soul of a chicken?
The Devil is prepared! -do your feel the flames a'lickin?

The Hunk of Funk

I tried the Funky Chicken
Cause I wanted to be cool
So I could have my pickin
Of all the chicks at school

I strutted and I bantered
As funky chickens do
So I could be the dancer
Admired by the brood

So I became impeccable
A classic piece of work
Unlike the other imbeciles
Who tried to do the Jerk

A Blessed Spirit

She is the unexpected rustle of the leaves
She is the witness to the hardwood trees
She is the shadows cast by fleeting birds
She is the calling, speaking not in words

She is the sunshine, bearing love itself
She is the scent that flowers by herself
She is the trickle underneath the brook
She is the necessary time it took to look

She is the earth, the very earth you plow
She is the sky behind the summer cloud
She is the faith that fosters all serenity
She is the grace of mountain's majesty

She is the robin that appears in spring
She is the reason for our very being

Malaise

Pushing up daisies, one by one
Just doesn't seem to be much fun
I want to be on top again
Unfettered, to naturally be free
To cultivate a flowered destiny
To spindle and bend
In wind and rain and sunny days
To bloom again and be amazed
And so I must contend
Pushing up daisies, one by one
Just doesn't seem to be much fun

www.ingramcontent.com/pod-product-compliance
Lightning Source LLC
LaVergne TN
LVHW061344060426
835512LV00016B/2657